Down Home in ARKANSAS

A Family Reunion Story

MARIA HOSKINS

Illustrated by Wade Hampton

C&V 4 Seasons Publishing Co.
Mayflower, Arkansas

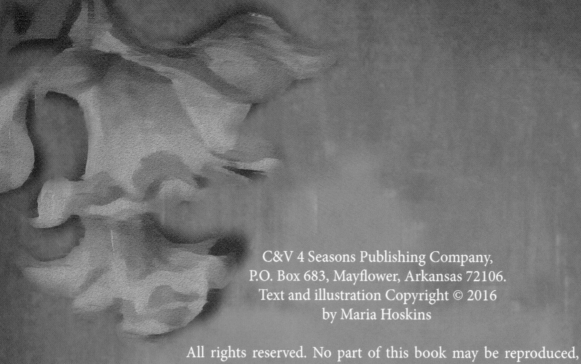

C&V 4 Seasons Publishing Company,
P.O. Box 683, Mayflower, Arkansas 72106.
Text and illustration Copyright © 2016
by Maria Hoskins

First Edition. Printed in USA

ISBN 978-0-9864036-2-0 hardback edition
ISBN 978-0-9864036-1-3 paperback edition
Library of Congress Control Number: 2016903967

Special thanks to Wade Hampton for bringing to life precious memories of reunions past in the illustrations created for this book. Many thanks to The Butler Center for Arkansas Studies, Central Arkansas Library System; Garbo Hearne, owner of Pyramid Art, Books, and Custom Framing, and her staff; Janis F. Kearney, author of the best-selling book *Cotton Field of Dreams;* and Patrick Oliver, literary consultant and author of *Turn the Page and Don't Stop,* for their guidance and support. Also, I would like to thank my webpage designer Julian White; book designer Denise Borel Billups; editor Gwendolyn Mitchell; and my church family for their support. I would like to thank my husband Archie; children Christina and Victoria; my mom Berthenia Gill and papa Alvin Gill; brother Freddy; and family and elders in the community who provided guidance, discipline and encouragement. A very special thanks to the Broyles-Collins family historians, Berthenia Gill and Leon Stanley. Most of all, thank you God for allowing me the opportunity to share and encourage students to write their stories, because "There is a story in all of us."

To the memory of
my Grandma Lillie Ella Collins, Grandpa Samuel Clark Collins Sr.,
and their children:
Joseph, Samuel, Walter Odus, Major, Mary,
Mamie, Joella, Wilma, Emma,
granddaughter Bertha and
my sister Wannette "Jeannie" Ryan.

To all connected to the Broyles-Collins family tree.

To my children, Christina and Victoria,
I pray that you recall heartfelt stories based on love
that will forever bring smiles to your faces
and joy to your hearts.

We are on our way to the old home place.

Folks are gathering from near and far.

It is time for our family reunion

down home in Arkansas.

My family travels from across the USA.

Some come in cars or vans, some travel in planes.

Our cousins come all the way from Oregon on a train.

This year my mother, papa, brother, and me

plan three days of family reunion activities.

Our family reunion is so much fun.
It doesn't matter what the weather,
cool and cloudy or hot days in the sun,
we love just being together.

We have a big family,
colorful like a rainbow you see.
In each generation you'll find
many shapes, sizes, colors, lots of diversity.

On the first night of our family reunion,
we have a "meet and greet."
We get together for welcomes and introductions,
for family history, entertainment,
and, of course, there is lots to eat.

My brother loves to sing.

He can sing, sway, and shout.

So much talent in our family—

singers, dancers, musicians, authors,

amazing people to learn about.

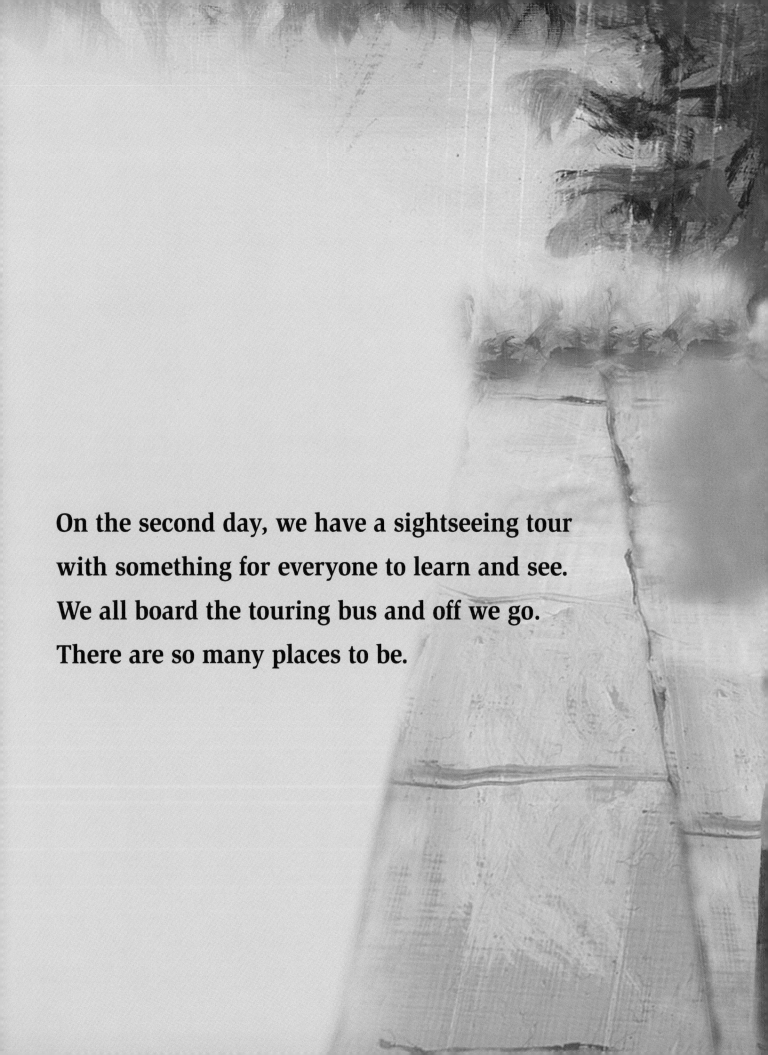

On the second day, we have a sightseeing tour
with something for everyone to learn and see.
We all board the touring bus and off we go.
There are so many places to be.

16

Stop one is the Discovery Museum.

All kids at heart get out to play.

Here learning is so much fun.

It's a perfect way to start the day.

Stop two is Pinnacle Mountain State Park.

From the overlook, we can see fields of tall corn stalks.

We learn about animals native to Arkansas.

We enjoy the river view and, just before lunch,

we go on a nature trail walk.

We drive by the Governor's mansion and
Arkansas State Capitol because
stop three is the Mosaic Templars Cultural Center
for a little Arkansas education.
We tour the Central High School Historic Site
and Museum where we learn about
"The Little Rock Nine"
and history of the
1957 desegregation.

One final stop on the tour and
the highlight our family will see
is the Clinton Presidential Library and Museum,
in honor of Arkansas's first presidential family.

We have a relaxing evening.
It's been a fantastic fun-filled day!
We eat more great food and
set up board games for everyone to play.
We share family stories and more history,
in our own special way.

It's Sunday morning and
our time is winding down.
We attend church together,
when our family comes to town.

Afterwards mother shares memories
and pictures of Grandma's farm.
Aunts, uncles, sisters, brothers, cousins,
the entire family gathers all around.

Now it's time for farewells and good-byes.
We hug, kiss, laugh, and cry.
Oh, what a great time we've had
so there is no reason to be sad.

We had fun
listening, learning, sharing, caring,
and just hanging out with family.
Down Home in Arkansas is a great place to be!

FAMILY REUNION FUN

Childhood memories stay with us all of our lives. I hope that my story gave you a glimpse of how a strong and loving family can create lifetime memories.

I have added this activity section so you will find a fun way to share family time, learn your family history, and learn a little about Arkansas or the history of your state.

I hope you plan to attend your family reunion and will learn more about your family history!

Facts About You

Name_____

Birthdate_____

Place of Birth_____

My mother and father _____

_____

_____

_____

Some of my favorite things to do _____

_____

_____

_____

_____

_____

What I most like about being a part of my family_____

_____

_____

_____

_____

_____

Family Tree

Family History Facts

What do you know about your relatives and family members? Why not share some interesting facts about your family and your family's history. Who are the special people in your family? Dates and places are always good to include if you have this information.

Here is what I know about...

Name_____

Birthdate_____ Place of birth_____

A little bit about them _____

_____

This is their relationship to me (Grandmother, Uncle, First cousin, etc.)

_____

Here is what I know about...

Name_____

Birthdate_____ Place of birth_____

A little bit about them _____

_____

This is their relationship to me (Grandmother, Uncle, First cousin, etc.)

_____

Here is what I know about...

Name_____

Birthdate_____ Place of birth_____

A little bit about them _____

_____

This is their relationship to me (Grandmother, Uncle, First cousin, etc.)

_____

Here is what I know about...

Name_____

Birthdate_____ Place of birth_____

A little bit about them _____

_____

This is their relationship to me (Grandmother, Uncle, First cousin, etc.)

_____

Here is what I know about...

Name_____

Birthdate_____ Place of birth_____

A little bit about them _____

_____

This is their relationship to me (Grandmother, Uncle, First cousin, etc.)

_____

Family Heirlooms and Treasures

What are some of the items that are important to your family? Tell a story about the history of this heirloom* or special treasure. Where did it come from? Was it made by a family member? Who owned it? Where is this treasure today? Do you have any personal memories about these items that you would like to share? Add pictures or drawings.

Note: Heirloom: A valuable object that has belonged to a family for several generations.

Home Sites

Who lived here?_____

Address_____

City_____

State _____

Zip _____

Who lived here?_____

Address_____

City_____

State _____

Zip _____

Who lived here?_____

Address_____

City_____

State _____

Zip _____

Who lived here?_____

Address_____

City_____

State _____

Zip _____

Favorite Family Recipes

Recipe for_____

Who cooked the recipe? _____

When or Occasion?_____

Recipe:_____

_____

_____

_____

_____

_____

_____

_____

_____

_____

_____

_____

_____

_____

_____

_____

Recipe for_____

Who cooked the recipe? _____

When or Occasion?_____

Recipe:_____

_____

_____

_____

_____

_____

_____

_____

_____

_____

_____

_____

_____

_____

_____

Recipe for_____

Who cooked the recipe? _____

When or Occasion?_____

Recipe:_____

_____

_____

_____

_____

_____

_____

_____

_____

_____

_____

_____

_____

_____

Recipe for_____

Who cooked the recipe? _____

When or Occasion?_____

Recipe:_____

_____

_____

_____

_____

_____

_____

_____

_____

_____

_____

_____

_____

_____

_____

_____

Favorite Family Photos

Tell us about your Favorite Family Reunions

Our family reunion was held in_____(city and town)

On these dates _____

Our theme for this reunion was_____

Here are some of the highlights_____

_____

_____

Our family reunion was held in_____(city and town)

On these dates _____

Our theme for this reunion was_____

Here are some of the highlights_____

_____

_____

Our family reunion was held in_____(city and town)

On these dates _____

Our theme for this reunion was_____

Here are some of the highlights_____

_____

_____

Documenting
Your Family Genealogy and History
A Few Tips to Get Started

1. Begin with what you already know—names of ancestors, places of residence, occupations, etc.

2. Verify your ancestor's place of residence by looking for names in public record archives in the city, county and state where they lived. An old phone book may also be a helpful tool.

3. Did they live in a home with other family members or friends of the family? Were they boarders, hired-hands, etc.?

4. Limit assumptions; look for proof—marriage(s), land ownership, tax records, etc.

5. Know the history of "their" history. Was schooling available? Was there a possibility of servitude or slavery?

6. Were any family members in the military? Did they serve during a particular wars?

7. What important historical events took place during their lifetime? Consider events like the Depression, Civil Rights movement, segregation, epidemics, illnesses, political changes, and other events as prompts to start conversations with elders and other family members.

8. Recognize that you are a part of your family history. Your story is important as well.

9. Who is you oldest living relative? What is their relationship to you?

10. Where does your family tree start? What are the names of these ancestors? Do you know how many generations of your family have descended from these ancestors?

(These questions were compiled using information contributed by:
The Butler Center for Arkansas Studies, Central Arkansas Library System)

Search websites like the ones listed here for
more information about researching your family history.

Ancestry for Genealogy, Family Trees and Family history records
www.ancestry.com

Family Search is a service provided by
The Church of Jesus Christ of Latter-Day Saints
https://familysearch.org/

Cyndi's List of Genealogy sites on the Internet
http://www.cyndislist.com/

The USGenWeb Project
http://usgenweb.org/

Arkansas Studies Institute and the ASI Research Portal
http://arstudies.org/

For additional information regarding assistance available through the
Butler Center for Arkansas Studies, Central Arkansas Library System,
visit www.butlercenter.org and www.cals.org

More about my family